GW00836538

HISTORIC DYES
No.1

THE HISTORY OF WOAD
AND
THE MEDIEVAL WOAD VAT

John Edmonds B.Sc.

First Edition 1998
Reprinted 2000

Copies available from the John Edmonds Publisher, 89 Chessfield Park, Little Chalfont, Buckinghamshire, HP6 6RX   England.
Phone 01494 762775

ISBN   0 9534133 0 6

'Omnes vero se Britanni vitro inficiunt, quod caeruleum efficit colorem, atque hoc horribiliore sunt in pugna adspectu'

Book v, xiv. The Emperor Julius Caesar's De Bello Gallico (54B.C.).

No mader, welde, or woad no litestere
Ne knew; the flees was of his former hewe;

The Former Age, Geoffrey Chaucer 1345-1400.

Acknowledgements

Numerous friends, colleagues and members of the public have over many years contributed assistance, ideas, corrections and inspiration which has made this booklet possible. In particular the help and facilities which has come from the management, staff and volunteers of the Chiltern Open Air Museum must be recorded. In addition a great debt is owed to Dr Peter Reynolds, director of the Butser Ancient Farm, Jill Goodwin, author and dyer, Dr Dominique Cardon, author of Guide des Teintures Naturelles and Professor Philip John, Head of Plant Sciences Laboratories at the University of Reading, and many others, whom space alone precludes from adding to this list. The opinions or deductions expressed in this booklet however remain the sole responsibility of the author.

Published by John Edmonds at 89 Chessfield Park, Little Chalfont, Buckinghamshire, HP6 6RX.   U.K.

Indigo from Woad: Before 1600 the only source of blue dye in Europe was woad. The woad was grown as a field crop and picked in its first year. It was then chopped up into a paste by a horse driven mill, then made into balls by hand. These were laid out to dry in the sun for about four weeks till they became hard like wood. The dried woad balls were broken up into a powder, sprinkled with water and allowed to ferment - this was known as couching.

When the couched woad was dry, it was packed into barrels ready for the dyer. The dyer poured hot water onto the couched woad in a vat and the water went black with the indigo from the woad. Indigo, however, is not soluble in water. The dyer had to add bran, yeast or beer together with lime. After three days fermentation the indigo was reduced to its soluble form. The dyer wetted the cloth and lowered it into the vat. As the cloth was lifted out, it slowly turned blue as the air oxidised the soluble indigo.   John Edmonds August 1995.

Contents

Preface

Following the establishment of a working dye-house at the Chiltern Open Air Museum, we are now publishing a series of histories and practical treatises on natural dyes using medieval and 18th. century recipes adapted from those used by professional dyers before the advent of synthetic dyes.

Throughout history professional dyers have experimented with all available dyestuffs and with great ingenuity had formulated fast dyes with a wide range of hues and brightness. The first synthetic dyes developed were amongst others, indigo, luteolin and alizarin which for centuries had been extracted from woad, weld and madder respectively.

The purpose in producing these booklets is to make available to students of textile dyeing and the general public, the history of a developing technology, giving practical details of the methods used and modern explanations where possible of the underlying principles.

Only recently has the microbiological basis of woad and Tyrian or Imperial Purple become the subject of modern scientific research. Subsequent booklets in this series will cover the other important plant and insect derived dyestuffs.

Introduction

Purple and blue must be the two most important colours in history. Imperial or Tyrian purple was derived from the gland of a sea mollusc, while the principle source of blue was indigo extracted from a variety of plants found in many different parts of the world.

It appears that every ethnic group around the world which has in the past produced textiles, has obtained indigo dye from one source or another. In Europe up to the end of the 16th. century it was the woad plant, Isatis tinctoria. Both purple and blue have a history leading back into prehistoric times. The ancient Phoenicians are credited with being the first people to exploit the Tyrian or Imperial purple, although it may have been first discovered by the Minoans of Ancient Crete.

Virtually the only natural blue dyestuff throughout history has been indigo. Woad was its source in Europe since Neolithic times, and it appears that the plant was introduced into Europe at the same time as farming spread from the Middle East and its only use was to dye cloth blue.

Both dyes are the most complex of all the natural dyes. The technique of vat dyeing, which was to ferment the dye to obtain its leuco or soluble form is common to both indigo and 6-6 dibromoindigotin which is the chemical name of imperial purple. Both dyes belong to the same homologous series. That is, they are chemical compounds that have the same functional groups but differ in formula by a fixed group of atoms. Their chemistry is similar and they undergo similar reactions.

Dyeing with Natural Dyes

It must not be assumed, that for professional dyers, dyeing in the middle ages, or at other times, was some sort of idyllic life, using just the natural products of the field and hedgerows, and avoiding all the noxious chemicals associated with modern synthetic dyes. In truth a number of dangerous and environmentally unfriendly chemicals were in common use, throughout recorded history. These were usually disposed of by pouring them on the ground, in the yard, in the street or in the nearest water course. There are a number of records of the antisocial behaviour of the dyers which caused protests.

Amongst the chemicals Rossetti(1) lists in his book of 1448, are arsenic, arsenic sulphide, lead, lead oxide, lead acetate, urine, sulphuric acid, asbestos and redoul (Coriara myrtifolia L.), the berries and leaves of which are toxic and which can produce poisonous fumes. In only one case does he warn of the dangers involved with these materials.

Plants were the main source of indigo while imperial purple could only be extracted from marine molluscs. Various purple coloured dyes can also be made from lichen and by mixing red and blue dyes but these are chemically unrelated to imperial purple. Surprisingly one particular marine mollusc Murex trunculus yields both indigo and dibromoindigotin to give a purplish/blue tint which is believed to be the origin of the biblical blue, referred to as Tekhelet in Hebrew.

The most comprehensive book on the history of woad was written in 1930 by Dr Jamieson B. Hurry entitled "The Woad Plant and Its Dye" (2). It was in fact published posthumously. Dr Hurry was a medical doctor in practice in Reading for many years before retiring to Bournemouth.

A modern account of woad and indigo and imperial purple is to be found in a more recent book in French "Guide des Teintures Naturelles"(3) by Dr Dominique Cardon published in 1990.

Hurry's book was carefully researched and gives a complete history of the medieval woad trade and a scientific explanation of the woad plant based of course on the state of knowledge in the 1930s. This book with its historical references is the starting point for any review of the history of woad dyeing.

A fundamental distinction exists between the use of woad grown in Europe before 1580 and that grown afterwards. Before 1580 the woad was grown for its indigo content. After 1600 the small amount of woad that continued to be cultivated was needed purely to assist in the fermentation of the imported, refined indigo. The woad vat continued to be used for this purpose. This was necessary until about 1890 in order to dissolve the indigo to leuco-indigo for the purposes of dyeing wool. The processed woad in the indigo/woad vat was merely the source of the fermenting medium which brings about the solution of indigo in the dyevat. The indigo content of the woad itself after 1600 was therefore unimportant. Certainly after 1600 woad was not always grown in areas of Britain where it had been previously grown. Woad was no longer imported in any quantity from those areas where it had once been the dominant crop. By at least 1820 other methods existed to dissolve indigo for dyeing cotton, but cloth dyed in an indigo/woad vat, known at the time as woaded cloth was considered superior to other methods particularly for wool until as late as 1930. It was said that it was the demand by the London Metropolitan police for woaded cloth for their uniforms which kept the woad industry going after 1900 albeit on a very reduced scale.

Dr Jamieson Hurry was well aware of the distinction between the medieval woad vat and the later woad-plus-indigo vat. The samples of woad balls collected by Dr Hurry from the last commercial batches of woad produced in 1929 still exist. These were given to Reading University by Dr Hurry, who for many years had close associations with that University. These were kept for exhibition to the undergraduates until woad ceased to be part of the agricultural curriculum. These are among the last commercially produced woad balls known still to be in existence(4)

It must be emphasised that the dye which is obtained from woad is indigo. World-wide there are some 30 to 40 species of unrelated plants which produce indigo and carry the precursors to indigo ih varying quantities. A precursor to indigo can even be detected in mammals.

The reason that plants produce indigo comes within the subject of Phyto-chemistry. Clearly indigo or its precursors have a function in the metabolism or protection of the plant. It probably gives the bitter taste to the plant and may act as an insecticide, ot at least a discouragement to ruminants.

In Europe, since the end of the 19th. century woad and natural indigo have been virtually replaced by chemically derived synthetic indigo.

It seems strange that woad which was second only to wine as an article of international trade in medieval times (5) has now faded not only from the consciousness of the general public, but from the knowledge of medieval historians and archaeologists. Until 1931 there were very few academic papers on the subject of woad and these were mostly written in the late 19th. century and probably owed their inspiration to the popular interest at that time in the new synthetic dyes. Before that, there were few books emanating from practical dyers, except those published in the USA.

Today however there is an increasing interest in natural dyes and the other possible uses of dye plants. In recent years valuable new historical research has been published by Dr Dominique Cardon on natural dyes in general and in her work on the procedure used for the medieval woad vat which she discovered in the archives of the Guild of the Arte Della Lana in Florence of 1418 and which she has translated into English and French. Today further research is being undertaken into the biochemistry, phytochemistry and botany of this fascinating plant.

Early Books on Natural Dyes

In the middle ages there are even fewer books on dyeing. One was the Plictho by Gioanventura Rossetti (1) written in 1548. The Plictho means the collection and was originally written in medieval Venetian dialect; its subtitle was "Instructions in the Art of the Dyers which Teaches the Dyeing of Woollen Cloths, Linens, Cottons and Silk by the Great Art as well as by the Common." Rossetti was the Master of the Arsenal in Venice. He states very clearly in the preface to his work that he had with great industry collected the dye recipes from the dyers and often paid for the information. The work had taken him 16 years. One of the dyestuffs he mentions is in fact woad, but unfortunately he fails to explain how it was used. He refers to it as this "ingenious art of great utility and benefit." With all his other dyes he is much more explicit. One suspects that the woad dyers were the least responsive to his enquiries.

The indigo extracted from the woad is a pigment, not a dye. In order to dye cloth the indigo must be dissolved and the technique used was in the medieval period a very closely guarded secret. The woad dyers had the advantage that the process was too complex to be explained except in terms of modern chemistry. Merely watching the dyers at work would not reveal the secret. The fermentation of the woad vat was dependant on maintaining a constant temperature over 30 hours and at a fixed alkalinity. If the temperature went too high or too low the fermentation stopped and throughout the fermentation an alkali would have to be added as the alkalinity drops as the fermentation continues. The dyers could not explain the process but acquired an empirical technique by long apprenticeship and experience. A written copy of the empirical recipe used by the Florentines in 1418 (5) has now been brought to light but it would be very difficult to follow the recipe without previous knowledge of the process. Alkalinity could not be measured accurately until the invention of the pH scale at the beginning of the 20th. century (6).

In the 18th. century considerable research was undertaken in France(7) to improve methods of dyeing. Dr Bancroft(8) who again was not a practising dyer carried out considerable research to find improved natural dyes.

The books written between 1790 and 1830 in the United States by Bemiss(9) and Partridge(10) and Asa Ellis(11) who were commercial dyers deal comprehensively with techniques used with the woad-indigo vat at that time. There was no comprehensive or accurate account of the woad vat used in Europe before 1600 until the discovery of the Florentine recipe of 1418.

The methods used in preparing the woad balls and couching the woad in the middle ages and later is very well documented. The old dyers frequently mention that the quality and indigo content of woad could vary greatly from season to season, and place to place, like the quality of wine, and for unspecified reasons.

The quality of the woad could only be determined by the final depth of colour achieved in the dyed cloth, and by the amount of cloth that could be dyed. Dyers in the past devised various methods to assist them in deciding the value of various consignments of woad.

As previously indicated good practical descriptions exist of the19th century indigo-woad vat. These however relied on adding concentrated imported indigo and used lime as the alkali and bran and madder to encourage fermentation.

Dr Hurry in his book speaks of the need for further research and investigation into the chemistry and technology of this remarkable trade.

The Etymology of Woad

Jamieson Hurry dealt extensively with this subject in his book, although he prefers to call it philology. The name of the woad plant is found in every European language and in various forms throughout history.

French (Languedoi)	La Guede	German	Der Weid
(Languedoc)	Le Pastel		
	Le Cocagne		
Italian	Guado	Dutch	Weeda
Medieval Latin	Gualdo	Spanish	Gualda
Roman Latin	Vitrum or Glastum	Czech	Vejt

The northern French word La Guede rhymes with woad. There are a number of French words where the equivalent English word has replaced the initial consonant "g" with "w" as in William from Guillaume and la guerre and war. If the Celtic trade in woad followed the etymology of the word then this should be evidence of an early trade in woad from Northern France. Julius Caesar in his commentaries on the Gallic Wars remarks on the extensive trading between Gaul and Britain.

Woad as a Celtic Cosmetic

As every English boy scout once knew, our British forebears are reputed on occasion to have daubed themselves with indigo derived from woad.

There are at least eleven separate references to woad and its use as a dye, pigment or cosmetic by classical authors Greek and Roman and also in Egyptian papyri.

The Archaeological Evidence

In addition to the literary evidence we have the archaeological. These two sources support each other. Indigo could be applied as a cosmetic either by daubing the skin or alternatively a more permanent and artistic finish could be obtained by tattooing the body. Both these techniques are referred to by the classical writers and we have first hand evidence of tattooing on the preserved skin of a Celtic chieftain of about 500 BC, excavated by Igor Rudenko (12) in the Alti region of Russia in about 1935. Tattooing presumably was a status symbol requiring some artistic and practical skills while daubing would be reserved for lessor mortals, as a temporary expedient.

The use of indigo presumably from woad appears to have been prevalent throughout the Celtic regions from Britain to Southern Siberia, as well as in the Eastern Mediterranean and Egypt.

The macerated leaf and seed pods of woad have been discovered in the Viking excavations in the Coppergate area of York and very recently in Iron Age deposits at Scunthorpe. It has been suggested that the very word Briton derives from a Celtic word indicating the "painted people."

What is seriously lacking in the archaeological record is any evidence of a Celtic dyehouse. This would perhaps be a simple rectangular construction leaving evidence of at least four post holes and the remains of a hearth over which an iron vat could heated. There could be evidence of the residue of the woad dumped nearby or at least the outer winged casing of the woad seed which seems the part most likely to survive.

The Medieval Woad Vat

In order to understand the use of woad in Celtic times it is necessary to digress into medieval dyeing. This process required the laborious processing of the woad leaves to preserve the indigo dye and to concentrate it sufficiently to be used commercially, on a large scale to produce dark blue cloth.

The process in essence was to grow the woad as a farm crop, grind the first year leaves into a paste in a woadmill, and make the macerated leaves into balls by hand as is necessary today. These are then laid out on racks to ferment and dry out.

Over a period of about four weeks the balls shrink to about a quarter of their size and a tenth of their weight. These are then broken up into a powder and fermented again by sprinkling the heaps with water. The heaps heat up spontaneously like garden compost but more vigorously. After about two weeks the heaps go cold and the woad looks like black tar. This can be dried out and stored. The dyestuff now contains about twenty times as much indigo as the same weight of fresh leaves. The problem for the dyer was that indigo is a pigment, not a dye. To use as a dye the indigo must be chemically reduced to its soluble form.

This can now be done with a reducing agent such as sodium dithionite. In medieval times this was done by again fermenting the processed woad. The so-called couched woad was placed in a vat, boiling water poured on it and the indigo appears like black ink, leaving the sludge at the bottom. To dissolve the indigo, the dyer added measured quantities of wood ash as an alkali and maintained a temperature of about 50 Degrees centigrade for 2 or 3 days. The pH of the vat is in fact critical to the process and the dyers devised empirical techniques to control it. The dissolved indigo is a greenish colour. The immersed cloth turns blue when exposed to the air.

To return to indigo as cosmetic. We have learned that ones hand rapidly stain to a semi permanent black as a result of manipulating the macerated woad into balls. One classical writer refers to Celtic women "the colour of Ethiopians", dyed for the purpose of some exotic display. This could possibly be done by rubbing the skin with freshly macerated woad leaves. Surprisingly pure powdered indigo mixed with water rubs off quickly as soon as it is dry. To daub oneself the indigo would need to be applied as a dye. This could be done provided the indigo is in its precursor form and before it has been oxidised to a pigment.

It seems a natural progression to try and preserve the chopped woad by squeezing it into hand size balls. Indigo cannot be extracted from woad leaves which have simply been left to dry. The closed, damp and partly anaerobic state existing within the woad ball does preserve the indigo.

To apply the blue colour to the skin as a war paint implies that the daub could be quickly applied and was available in large quantities. It seems that the only way this could be done would be to skim the surface patina from the surface of a fermenting woad vat. and apply this to the face. This would be a mixture of pure indigo together with some unoxidised dissolved indigo. Caesar in his commentaries gives no indication of how the war paint was made and applied, other than to say it was derived from woad. If these deductions are correct it would indicate that woad vats similar to those used in the middle ages were common as early as the iron age in Celtic Europe.

Woad Dyeing in the Saxon and Viking Period

In recent years evidence has been excavated in London revealing Anglo-Saxon textile fragments of wool, linen and silk which had been dyed with madder, weld and woad to give patterned cloth. Silks have been found which were woven abroad. It appears Pavia in Italy was regularly visited by Anglo-Saxon merchants and pilgrims from the end of the 8th. century.

Work done by Frances Pritchard (25) at the London Museum and by Scandinavian archaeologists clearly establishes the sophistication of Anglo-Saxon and Viking weaving and dyeing. The techniques of tablet weaving of borders and selvedges with twill and plain weaving designs have all been recorded in the archaeology of those times.

In the period 867 to 954 A.D. Yorvik (York) was the capital of a Viking state and Coppergate was the industrial area of that city. In recent years, from the York Archaeological Trust convincing evidence has come to light of the use of woad and madder from the deposits of woad residues left after dyeing in the Coppergate district. "The cloth fragments (from Coppergate) all appear a dull brown colour when excavated and cleaned; laboratory analysis is required to prove that they were originally a blaze of colour. Reds, greens, blues and blacks and all shades in between could be produced using a range of natural dye substances such as the plants madder(red), weld(yellow) and woad(blue), either singly or in combination".

In addition concentrations of the very small seeds of the weld plant (Reseda luteola) have been found. The indications are that in Viking Coppergate commercial dyeing with madder, weld and woad was a well established industrial process. Normally madder and weld require a mordant such as alum to form a fast dye. It has not yet been identified directly what mordant they were using, but club moss, Lycopodium complanatum was found associated with the deposits of madder. The biological accumulation of aluminium in this plant has been measured. One percent of the metal aluminium has been extracted. Other mosses contain less of the metal. It seems probable that this plant was imported for the use of the dyers. This clubmoss is virtually unknown in Britain but is indigenous to Scandinavia.

Medieval Dyes

The three most important dyestuffs used in Europe in the Medieval period were madder, weld and woad. Of these the woad was economically the most important and its cultivation was widespread across Europe. Geoffrey Chaucer's poem, "The Former Age" written about 1380 recalls a mythical former age when people were free of vanity and avarice and when the dyer (litestere) knew nothing of madder, weld or woad, and cloth remained the colour of the fleece :-

> Ne mader, welde or woad no litestere
> Ne knew; the flees was of its former hewe

There were of course many other dyes in use in Chaucer's day, but madder, weld, (or Dyer's Rocket) and woad, giving red, yellow and blues respectively together with various browns and blacks were the dyes available to the common people throughout Europe. At one time crimson and scarlet were reserved by Sumptuary laws to the various ranks of the nobility. These were in any case extremely expensive and were derived from insects such as kermes and Polish cochineal.

The woad dyers were the elite of the profession and normally specialised in this one dyestuff. The medieval woad process was the most complex of the dye processes, involving controlled fermentation.

The Cultivation of Woad

Woad (Isatis tinctoria) has been grown in Europe since the Iron Age and almost certainly as far back as the Neolithic period when farming first appeared in Europe. Seeds of other dye plants such as weld were discovered in the archaeological excavations on the Lake of Zurich in Switzerland. Woad, like madder however is not indigenous to Europe. It is a Mediterranean biennial which originated in Turkey and the Middle East. Woad was grown extensively in Europe as a cultivated field crop until the end of the 16th. and the beginning of the 17th. Century. It continued to be grown in England at least, until the early years of the 20th. Century on a greatly reduced scale. Dyers during this period continued to use the couched woad as the fermenting medium for the imported indigo in the woad vat. Increasingly from about 1800 other methods using concentrated acid, iron sulphate and zinc for cotton dyeing,and finally in about 1890 sodium dithionite was used as the reducing agent for indigo.

Although only the species of woad know as Isatis tinctoria, appears to have been used in Europe as the source of indigo dye, in Turkey there are reputed to be some thirty to forty different species of woad growing wild and each with its own local habitat (13). These range over the whole extent of Turkey. There does not seem to be any published information on the indigo content of these various wild woads.

Some research has been carried out in recent years at the Plant Sciences Dept. of Reading University into the arable cultivation of woad, and its possible adaptation as a set-aside crop. This crop was largely obsolete before modern crop science commenced in about the 1840's.

Several of the old writers on woad emphasise the variability in quality of the woad. The indigo content of the leaves could be dependent on a number of factors, since the precursors to indigo in the woad leaf is there presumably primarily as an insecticide to protect the plant. Certainly the indigo percentage of dry weight appears to be the same regardless of the fertility of the soil. The size and quantity of leaves produced however is clearly dependent on fertility.

In Saxon and medieval times the woad production was concentrated in the southern and western counties of England, particularly in Somerset, Dorset and Hampshire. In the 18th. century when the indigo content of woad was less important (since imported indigo was being added to the woad vats) cultivation moved to the midlands and eventually to the fenland areas of Lincoln.

In an old recipe of the 18th century, it states the woad balls are the size of a "ferthing luv" which it has been suggested was probably a "farthing loaf" in a Somerset accent.

The main areas for woad growing in Europe in the medieval period when the indigo content of the woad was important were:-

France - Toulouse, Picardy   Germany - Cologne, Erfurt
Northern Italy   Spain.

The Medieval Woad Industry in England

In the medieval period in Europe processed woad developed into a major item of international commerce. Its impact on the economies of several countries on the continent of Europe was far greater than in Britain.

It is clear from the records that trade and industry, and the financial resources of a merchant class to support it, were late in starting in England; compared with the rest of Europe. In the 11th. 12, and 13th centuries, virtually the only major export from Britain was wool fels and fleeces. The manufacture of textiles in

England to a standard capable of competing with the manufacturing centres on the Continent did not arrive until the 15th and 16th. centuries. Until then, the export of wool fleeces was "a pillar of the state" and "the chief wealth of this nation". As a symbol of this the Lord Chancellor of England sat on a wool sack as his official seat in the House of Lords.

Fortunately English wool was highly regarded on the Continent and Italian merchants in particular would buy the fleeces direct from the sheep breeders. Wool was "bought forward" in bulk and collected months later after shearing(14) The ledgers of Italian merchants were accepted as proof positive of debts in English courts of Law. On one occasion the Crown jewels were in pawn to Italian merchants for money lent to the King and of course the Bank of England is still situated in Lombard Street. Fortunes were made from the export of wool but the intrinsic value of unworked wool was very much less than the finished textiles.

Cloth was made in England before 1300, but high quality cloth was normally imported. Considerable quantities of inferior woollen cloth was exported to Italy, reworked, fulled and dyed and reimported to England as superior cloth. This economic weakness was appreciated at the time and increasingly efforts made to encourage the manufacture of high quality woollen cloth in England, to the extent that by about 1350 the export of raw wool was for a period made illegal. The efforts made by the English authorities to encourage foreign artisans to settle here were greatly assisted by the religious and politically inspired persecution in Europe. Foreign textile craftsmen were given various incentives such as tax relief to settled in England.

Why English wool was so much in demand is unclear. Wool was of course produced over most of Europe and English wool then as now varies enormously from the very coarse wool, suitable for carpets to long staple wool used for worsteds and short staple for woollens. It may have been that due to the damp climate and abundant grass the English wool took the natural dyes then available, particularly woad, more satisfactorily than Continental wool. Or possibly with a more equable climate the sheep were less stressed resulting in a more uniform quality of wool. Certainly it was not until the 17th. century that the fine merino wool from Spain became more important. By then dyeing with indigo derived from woad had been superseded by the more convenient and popular imported tropical indigo.

In 1551 Flemish weavers and dyers were allowed to settle at Glastonbury on monastic land. There the monastic brewhouse and bakehouse were allotted to the dyers. The increase in dyeing at that period resulted in an increased demand for woad, weld, madder. All these commodities were now beginning to be produced in Britain.

It is recorded that the keeper of Worcester Gaol in the 1580's employed poor prisoners on woad growing on 30 acres of land near the city. At the same time an attempt was made to grow woad in Ireland by the English undertakers in the 1580's. Civil turmoil evidently brought it quickly to an end. Woad was also imported into Southampton from the Azores towards the end of the 16th. century.

The amount of woad grown in England can be estimated for 12 southern counties in 1586 as 4910 acres. This would yield about 600 tons of couched woad ready for the dyers. This is at a time when the total amount imported was of the order of 20,000 tons. There was however considerable interest in growing woad in England(15) English woad would appear to have accounted for about 3% of the market. It was a profitable crop if well grown and properly processed. There was a technical reason why the best quality woad could not be supplied on a consistent basis from English sources: Britain has a very damp and rainy climate, brought in by the prevailing south westerly winds from the Atlantic. The woad needs to be dried as rapidly as possible in the form of woad balls. If the weather is wet the balls dry very slowly and become mouldy and even fly blown. The colour of the balls is mildewy compared with those from the Continent. French woad from Toulouse was considered the best available on the London market.

The Woad Trade in France

The two great woad growing regions in France were Picardy and the region of Lanquedoc between Toulouse, Albi and Carcassonne.

Woad Production in Picardy

In 1986 M.Delost(16) provided an account of the woad trade in Picardy in NW France, based on the municipal records of the City of Amiens. This covered the period 1377 - 1499. During this period in particular, the production and processing of woad was a major industry of the region.

The towns of Abbeville, St Quentin and Amiens were the principal woad markets in Picardy. All these towns lie on the banks of the River Somme. The river was the highway to the sea and the annual woad crop preserved as woad balls or as couched woad was transported down river to the port of Le Crotoy at the mouth of the Somme. The City of Amiens was able to impose a tax on the export of woad.

The main woad growing region corresponded roughly to the region of Amiens (the Pagus Ambianensis) but some books state that the main region was to the south of the River Somme, while De Peerck in his Medieval Cloth Trade in Flanders and Artois reports that woad was also brought from Albert, to the North East of Amiens. Towns of lesser importance such as Nesle also served as markets.

The woad trade became concentrated in Amiens in two ways. Firstly, the producers brought their woad to the town where the towns people arranged for its export, and secondly the merchants of Amiens went out to collect the woad. The citizens had no option but to pass through the town and hence pay the municipal taxes, although efforts were made to avoid it. Similar tax collecting methods were used all over Europe. We know this was done at the Bargate at Southampton and Geoffrey Chaucer, the father of English literature, was at one time, the controller of customs at London's Bishops Gate.

The first stage in the preparation of the woad consisted in washing and then grinding the woad in the mills to macerate the fresh leaves into a paste. These mills were very common in the woad growing regions and in the immediate approaches to Amiens. Some that are known are the mills at St Jean to the SW of the town, St Pierre, to the NE and Cagney, to the SE. The first two belonged to the town and were rented out to small merchants or artisans. Al least one mill was privately owned. There must have been many others.

The second stage or couching of the woad (or conrage in French) was carried out by people known as les Conreurs. The woad balls were crushed, dampened with water, then left to ferment. It was then left to dry, ground up and sieved and packed in barrels. The Conreurs were semi independent artisans who were paid to process the woad entrusted to them by the merchants.

The local consumption of woad appears to have been small. One finds at the end of the 14th. century five or six dyers using each about 2 or 3 barrels of couched woad per year. In 1454 there were 7 dyers using 52 barrels of woad. The consumption rose during 1480-1490 when economic improvement and new textile manufacturing came to Amiens.

The woad prepared in Amiens was mainly for export. From 1377 to 1429 on average 1114 barrels were exported each year, while from 1431 to 1490 only 350 each year on average.

Where the exported woad went to is rarely indicated in the records. It is estimated that most of the woad was sent down the River Somme to the coast. The port of Le Crotoy situated at the mouth of the Somme was endowed with an anchorage in 1398. Despite attempts by the Amiens merchants to avoid it, it is estimated that at least three quarters of the woad exported in the following years passed through the anchorage, and most of that must have gone to England, Calais and Flanders. The land route to the north went to Artois and Flanders and in a small measure to Paris and Rouen.

The export trade in Amiens was controlled by local merchants. Strangers were rare, and the business they did was small on average. The exporter, Colart Daut, citizen of Brugge, mentioned in 1438 to 1463 and at other times was in fact the son of an Amiens family.

In Amiens itself, the trade was not well organised. None of the companies involved in the trade were comparable in size with the Italian companies at that time. There were about 700 woad exporters belonging to some 40 family businesses which existed only for a limited period of one season or for several expeditions. These were often family syndicates which reformed each year. They were small concerns and the partnerships were not exclusive. One merchant could act on his own or in another group.

In 1218 the principal merchants in Amiens formed one organisation called the "Douzaine". This was a kind of chamber of commerce to defend the interests of the merchants against the municipality or the king.

The merchants and their companies rarely specialised in woad, but traded in a range of commodities. These would include wine, cloth, corn, etc. The merchants themselves came from all walks of life and were engaged in many other activities besides trading. They included many wealthy citizens, but also artisans, butchers, pastry cooks, innkeepers, hoteliers, bakers, brewers, tanners, shoemakers, dyers, hosiers, masons, workers in pewter, barristers, attorneys and judges. For all these people woad represented a profitable speculation rather than a regular activity.

This type of family enterprise was not unique to Northern France and it can be imagined as the natural beginnings of business which lead eventually to the joint stock companies, limited liability and the vast business corporations of the modern world. As M. Delost indicated business organisation in Italy was much more advanced, but even there business empires were controlled by the founder or his immediate family.

As for the big wholesale merchants, they combined the income obtained from the export of woad with other activities such as life annuities, income from real estate, rents from town properties or royalties.

From the municipal records it is clear that there was a profound crisis in the export of woad in 1430 from which it never properly recovered. Exports fell to 200 barrels in 1436, increased to 700 barrels in 1444, and then finally ceased altogether.

There was a number of reasons for this failure. In 1429 war started again between the Duke of Burgundy and the Dauphin. The Treaty of Arras of 1435 annexed the towns of the Somme region to the Duke of Burgundy. There was antagonism between Burgundy and the English, and as a result Amiens was unable to trade with the Low Countries. The siege of Crotoy in 1436 was largely responsible for the catastrophic decline in trade in that year. The return of peace eventually allowed the recovery of 1444. However the combination of competition from new woad production areas and the effects of the war dealt the final blow to the trade of Amiens.

A lasting memorial to the influence and prosperity of the woad trade in Amiens is to be found high up on the south wall of its cathedral overlooking the narrow street. This is the statue depicting two woad merchants of the 13th. century displaying their wares. The woad merchants paid towards the cost of erecting the great cathedral.

Woad Production in Toulouse

Contemporaneously with these developments, the woad trade flourished to an even greater extend in the city of Toulouse and the surrounding area. The Toulouse woad in the 16th. century was considered the best, by the London dyers(20). This region was the origin of the mythical land of cocagne, a land flowing with milk and honey. The cocagne de pastel were the woad balls. It has been estimated that there were 500 - 700 woad mills in operation in the Toulouse region of France.Even today a few of the magnificent town houses built by the woad merchants still exist. At the beginnibg of the 16th. century some 200.000 bales of woad were transported along the River Garonne for export from Bordeaux. Much of this, together with cargoes of wine were destined for the English market. At various times when England and France were at war special licence was granted for English merchant ships to collect the valuable woad from Bordeaux. The great woad merchants made fortunes from the trade, but the cultivation and processing of the woad was very labour intensive with the result that many others shared in the prosperity. At one time Toulouse was able to purchase its freedom from the Kings of France and had its own parliament as a separate state. By the end of the 16th. century the good times were over. Trade was extending all round the world. Increasingly, refined indigo was coming into

Europe inspite of great opposition from the woad trade. This came from the tropical indigofera plant and was much cheaper and easier for the dyers to use.

The Medieval Textile Trade in Italy

The recipe for the woad vat of 1418 belonging to the Guild of the Arte Della Lana is apparently the only complete recipe for a medieval woad in existence.

The late Middle Ages, a period of technical and cultural innovation, culminated in the Italian Renaissance. The great wheel had replaced the hand spindle for spinning in every cottage and the horizontal looms had replaced the old vertical looms. These both increased production and in the case of the horizontal looms, it made possible the use of the figure harness to recreate the repeated patterns of fine brocades, in place of the hand embroidery immortalised in the Bayeaux Tapestry. In Venice, Verona, Padua and elsewhere, the art of reworking and finishing cloth was brought to perfection. These included besides brocades, silks, velvets and "felvets super felvets." The invention of water-driven fulling mills allowed increased production of broadcloth. This was woollen cloth woven with the simple tabby weave but heavily fulled and felted. Today this cloth is usually seen on billiard tables, tennis balls and officers' dress uniforms. The wealth of the Medicis was founded on cloth and gave rise to the banking system in Europe. By the sixteenth century the Banco di San Giorgio, founded in 1407 was the most important credit institute in Europe. The Strada Nuova, the street in Genoa lined with Renaissance palaces still exists. The most prestigious of these was the home of Tobia Pallavicino, active in the foreign affairs of the Genoese Republic and head of a financial empire based on the alum trade, which the Italians also controlled. Alum was an essential mordant for madder, weld and other natural dyes. Such men commissioned the architecture and paintings which now for us epitomise the glory of Renaissance Italy.

Venice and Genoa again, were the centres from which in the fourteenth century the fleets of great galleys sailed to Constantinople and Acre in the Levant to connect with the caravans arriving from the East. Each autumn the so called Flanders Fleet arrived in Southampton.

The Great Galleys were the express packet service of the medieval period. Come calm or high water the galleys would arrive on schedule. The oarsmen were freemen of the city of Genoa. The archers on these ships were chosen by public competition. The galleys happily were not rowed all the way from Italy to England, but were lateen rigged and rowed only when the wind was not set fair or on entering and leaving harbour. The arrival of the Flanders Fleet at Southampton

Statue of two woad merchants of the 13th century
on the south wall of the cathedral at Amiens, Picardy

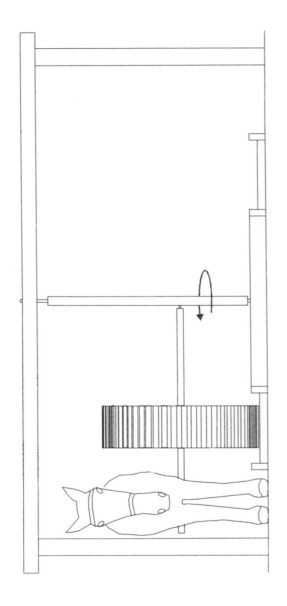

A Typical Horse Driven Medieval Woad Mill

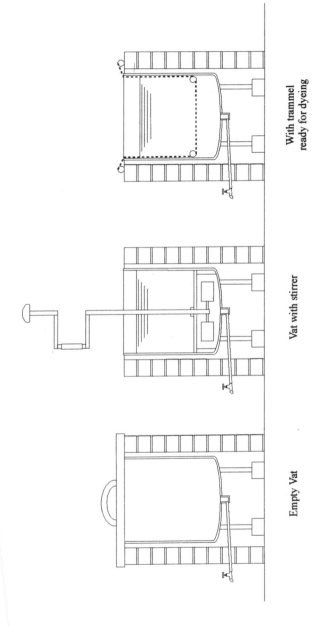

Empty Vat

Vat with stirrer

With trammel
ready for dyeing

Replica of a Victorian Woad Vat

was the social event of the year. The Captain of the fleet would entertain kings and ambassadors in style on his flag ship, equipped with costly plate and furnishings. Music was supplied by the Captain's musicians.

The crews would peddle the cargo or rampage in the streets of Southampton as the mood took them. The first Venetian ambassador was appointed to the Court of St.James in 1319 following complaints from the citizens of Southampton. The illuminated commission appointing Cristoforo Duodo as captain of the Flanders galleys in 1472 is to be found in the Bodleian library. The "Galley Captayn" was accompanied by a priest, a notary, two physicians, four musicians and two or three personal servants. Each galley was commanded by a Patrone who was usually a Venetian or Genoese aristocrat. Each ship had 170 oarsmen, 30 bowmen, a navigating officer, purser, a caulker and carpenters, cook, cellarman and minor officials. The crew would total more than 200 souls. The galleys could carry about 140 tons of freight. In 1470 woad was the second biggest import into Southampton. Wine was the biggest and weld the third most important. Southampton at that time rivalled London as the main port of entry. The wool clip from the Cotswolds went out as the return cargo.

It has been said that by the thirteenth century, trade and manufacture could now properly be termed commerce and industry. The ledgers of the Italian merchants were accepted as proof of contracts in the English courts of law and the wool crop was subject to a futures market. The Flemish textile industry was for many years dependant on English wool.

The Medieval Tapestries

The technique used in weaving the "haute-lisse" tapestries required the weaver to sit facing the back of tapestry. The outline of the design would have been marked on to the warps, but to check the detail of the design the weaver would refer to a full-size painting or cartoon of the finished design. This was placed behind the weaver but reflected in a mirror placed in front of him but on the other side of the warps. He would have to peer through the warps to see the reflection of the cartoon in the mirror and to compare it with his work.

In the Middle Ages the design was not normally made by the weaver. The mythological or religious subjects of the tapestry would be decided on in consultation with a scholar or cleric. He would take a theme and supply the information or explanation to allow an artist to draw and paint the full-size cartoon. This was normally drawn on linen. Later they were drawn on paper. Occasionally existing illustrations such as illuminated manuscripts were copied. In the case of contemporary scenes, the artist would have much more a free hand in composing the picture. This appears to have happened in the case of the Devonshire tapestries, exhibited at the Victoria and Albert Museum in London. This series of large tapestries date to about 1540.

The preoccupations of the wealthy and usually educated classes in the early Middle Ages is represented in the tapestries. The scenes depict romantic love, the lives of the saints, classical and mythological scenes, allegories and famous battles, ancient and contemporary. Others occasionally illustrate hunting scenes and a detached curiosity with the activities of the labouring classes. There are also scenes of ladies and gentlemen playing musical instruments and disporting themselves in sylvan glades surrounding by birds, flowers and fruits.

For many reasons medieval tapestries are important historical records. In particular they are virtually the only fabrics, more than three hundred years old, to survive in reasonable condition. Tapestries required great skill and were always extremely expensive. They were intended to grace the walls of castles and ecclesiastical buildings, and were the property of the great and famous. They were normally protected from wear, sunlight or washing. Fabrics of any description were in the past comparatively expensive and clothing in particular passed down the social classes and were worn to destruction.

The natural dyes used in medieval tapestries were normally limited to madder, weld or woad separately or in combination. Other dyes were of course available but they were rare and even more expensive. The wefts, the threads seen on a tapestry were woollen yarn. The hidden warps were usually linen thread. All dyes will fade to some degree. The natural dyes fading much more than modern synthetic dyes. Dyed clothes when washed were frequently redyed to a darker colour. Tapestries were not washed but over the centuries have inevitably faded. It is rare to see yellow or green on a medieval tapestry. Yellow is the first to fade. Green becomes blue, yellow turns to a white. The reds fade to a degree but the blues will be as good as the day they were dyed. Indigo, whether from woad, as was the case in European dyeing before about 1580, or from any other source of indigo is one of the fastest of natural dyes.

The overall impression of a medieval tapestry is of the dominant blue. Grass and leaves were in the past green as they are today, but the green is now blue. The colours of the newly woven tapestries were bright and distinctive and even strident to modern taste. To assume the present state of the colours of the tapestries were representative of medieval taste is as historically incorrect as to assume that all Victorians wore sepia coloured clothes.

Throughout the ages, colours have been the subject of fashion in the same way as design. Colours popular in the 18th. century were different from those 100 years later. The story is repeated with the introduction of refined imported indigo to replace woad dyeing, the use of Bow dye, the brilliant red of the British army, chosen soon after its introduction as a very fashionable colour of the 1640's, and the instant popularity of Perkin's mauveine in the 1860's.

There is a case to be made for museums to display reproductions of medieval tapestries in their original colours using their original dyestuffs. In the same way as there are those amongst us who prefer to see Shakespearean plays in 16th. century costume and find modern costume a distraction from what Shakespeare and his audiences expected. If we wish to see medieval tapestries as examples of medieval thought, fashion and technical skills then they need to be seen in their true colours. It is not possible to restore a tapestry by cleaning to its originally appearance, but copies can be made which would be more faithful than the examples which have survived.

To quote Mr A.F. Kendrik (17) "On occasions of special rejoicing, large stores of the richest tapestries were sometimes brought forth to cover the walls of churches or dwellings, both inside and out. For state ceremonial, victories, pageants and tournaments, their brilliant colours enlivened the buildings and streets." To us however, they can give only a very faded impression of the beliefs, studies, wars and rustic toil, the sports and amusements, the costumes and amusements and manners of times past.

The Chemistry of the Woad Vat

Elijah Bemiss(9) makes the remark in his book of 1806 (p.134) :- "Those that read this chapter with attention, will not be surprised that the masterpiece for apprentices to dyers of the great dye, is, to set the woad vat and work her."

Even after 500 years of fading the quality of woad dyeing achieved on wool in the tapestries and embroideries by the medieval dyers is self evident. The question is, how was this achieved with the technology then available?

From a number of sources we are able to reconstruct the basic requirements of the medieval woad vat. But there were some differences in techniques and ingredients between various centres of dyeing. France, Italy and Flanders were all at various times centres of manufacture of high quality textiles. High quality dyeing would have been an essential factor in their production.

We have very little information on cheap textiles. There was in England a type of course cloth known as Burrel. However none seems to have survived and there seems to be no descriptions of it.

A celebrated book was published in 1548 called The Plictho (1) by Gioanventura Rossetti. In this book there is a list of some 20 dyestuffs used by the commercial dyers in Venice at that time. Woad is included amongst these. Unfortunately very little information is given in the book on woad dyeing. Dr Cardon has informed me of a number of other French and Italian sources on medieval woad dyeing. To deal with the subject comprehensively, clearly all these references require study.

It is reported that woad still grows wild in the Rhine valley in Germany on steep and dry slopes(18). This appears similar to the environment which exists in the Seven valley at Tewkesbury in England where naturalised uncultivated woad has also been located.

The degree of alkalinity is critical to the fermentation process in order to bring about the reduction of the indigo to form soluble indigo. Without a pH scale, which was not introduced until 1909 by S.P. Sorenson(19) alkalinity could not be precisely measured. Also in England since the end of the 16th. century woad ceased to be used as the main source of blue dye. All the vats of which we have details after this date rely on added indigo in the woad vat "to give a more orient colour(20)".

At the Chiltern Open Air Museum, for our experimental "medieval" woad vat of equivalent strength we used more woad to replace the added indigo which they were using in the 18th. and 19th. centuries. The 17th. century dyers had greatly reduced the amount of woad used in the vats when the imported indigo became available. By then it appears the woad was used mainly to provide a fermenting medium and the dyers relied on the added indigo to provide the colour.

For experimental purposes we used an electrically heated and temperature controlled vat of 30 litres capacity. The basic ingredients are as suggested by Elijah Bemiss(9) in 1806, namely:-

Couched woad	5 pounds
Water	30 litres
Madder	100 gms
Bran	100 gms
Alkali	wood ash or slaked lime

We believe the medieval dyers relied on repeated immersions into the vat to obtain the deeper blues. This technique is confirmed by the old descriptions with the first immersion corresponding to a pale blue, a middle blue with the second, and a deep blue with the third immersion. Strangely enough, it is more difficult to obtain an even and satisfactory very pale blue in a strong vat. A pale colour is best obtained from a strong vat from which most of the dye has already been extracted.

The first question to be decided was at what temperature the vat should be held, to obtain optimum reduction of the indigo leeched from the woad. William Partridge(10) is very explicit on this point. He states the vat should be between 45 and 50 Deg. C. This is much higher than one expects with fermentation. For an enzymatic process a temperature of 37 Deg. C. would seem to be more appropriate.

The second question which arises is what degree of acidity or alkalinity is optimum to convert the indigo to its soluble form by fermentation in the woad vat to allow the fabric to take up the dye.

In the Devonshire tapestries of 1450 in the Victoria & Albert Museum in London there are three well defined shades of blue dye which are a dark navy blue, a middle blue and a light blue. There is a distinct difference between the shades of blue derived from woad and the blue shades derived from the indigofera and the polygonums. The 16th century London dyers spoke of obtaining a brighter or "more orient blue" from imported indigo. A close inspection of the Devonshire tapestries also reveals a shade of pink or green mixed with the blue. With indican derived indigo (as opposed to the Isatin B precursor in woad) the colours obtained are pure blues. With couched woad these extraneous tints of pink and green are to some extent unavoidable. This does however indicate a method of identifying medieval couched woad dyed cloth from later indigo dyed cloth. The difference lies in the impurities. Interestingly, recently a technique has been suggested for differentiating between synthetic and natural indigo using Carbon 14 Dating techniques which would reveal the fossil origin of the carbon in the molecules of the synthetic indigo.

Several of the classical authors refer to the Celts dyeing their skin. From our experience they could have obtained a durable blue stain with a mixture of the pure indigo pigment existing on the surface of the vat mixed with the dissolved indigo in the woad vat. In a well conditioned woad vat this could have been obtained by skimming the surface off the top of the vat.

The preparation of the woad for the dyers involved three separate procedures:-

1. The leaves were collected, then macerated in a mill and made into balls. The balls were then laid out on airing racks for about 4 weeks (depending on the weather) until they shrank and became as hard as pieces of wood. It is interesting to note that if woad leaves are simply dried, the precursor to the indigo is altered such that it is not possible to extract indigo. The preservation of the woad in the form of woad ball is necessary in order to produce the indigo.
2. The balls were then ground into a powder passed through a sieve and then they were dampened with water and left in heaps for 2 weeks to ferment. The heaps were regularly turned and raked. This encourages further and even fermentation and renders the woad into a condition such that the sludge drops to the bottom of the vat and does no contaminate the dissolved indigo in the vat above the sludge,.
3. Finally the dried couched woad was placed in the vat with lime or wood ash and boiling water was poured into the vat. After stirring, the temperature dropped to 50 Deg.C. It was held at this temperature for 30 hours for fermentation and the reduction of the indigo to leuco indigo to proceed. From our experience a vat pH of 8.5-9 would have been the optimum. If the alkalinity is higher than 9 then the fermentation stops, and if it is below 7 the sludge floats to the top of the vat.

It appears that when the leaves are first macerated the sap in the plant leaves is mixed intimately with the plant bacteria and their enzymes. This results in a break down of the sap into glucose and indigo. The woad however remains alkaline or neutral with very little increase in acidity.

What happens during couching is less clear. We know that the reaction is exergonic and the temperature rises to about 50 Deg.C. and noxious fumes are given off. Again there is very little increase in acidity.

Finally in the vat a patina of pure indigo forms on the surface from the redissolved indigo or leuco-indigo in the liquid. The leuco-indigo fixes itself to the immersed fabric and reforms as indigo on the cloth when it has been exposed to the air.

Bran and/or madder were sometimes added to the vat. The purpose of this was probably to further deplete the vat of dissolved oxygen and assist in extracting oxygen from the indigo molecules.

The Ingredients of the Medieval Woad Vat

Throughout medieval Europe the basic chemistry of the woad vat must have remained the same. We know from extant medieval tapestries and embroideries which colours they were able to produce.

A woad vat in medieval times could be maintained at a constant temperature by a variety of methods. A large insulated vat would lose its temperature only slowly. In the case of metal vats a wood fire could be used under the vat. With wooden vats the water could be partial removed, reheated and returned to the vat. To control the pH of the vat without modern electronic equipment presents another problem.

Bemiss(9) gives three methods to control the alkalinity of the vat which were presumably used in conjunction with each other. These were :-

a) By feel - if the liquid is rubbed between thumb and finger, it feels slippery if alkaline, and rough if neutral or acidic.

b) By smell - although the smell for many people is objectionable, there is a subtle change in smell depending on alkalinity.

c) By use of sample dyeing. If a small sample cloth is immersed, on lifting out of the vat the initial green colour can appear dull or bright evidently again depending on the alkalinity.

A further method mentioned in the literature was "by taste on the tongue giving a pungent taste". These techniques would require great skill and experience to give consistent results. The same techniques are reported to have been used in Morocco as late as the beginning of this century.

In Southern France "re-cooked wood ash" (3) was used as an alkali for the woad vat. This consisted of vine wood ash mixed with the dregs of the wine vats.

A Chemical Explanation of the Medieval Woad Process

Referring to recent research carried out by Professor Ortwin Meyer(21) at Bayreuth University and by Professor Philip John at Reading University it is now possible to follow the biochemical process in extracting and transferring to cloth. This was the basis of woad dyeing in Medieval Europe

The fresh first year woad leaf possesses two precursors to indigo. The source of the indigo is about 20% indican (a glucoside) and 80% isatan B (a ketoglutinate). If woad leaves are dried either by

1) allowing them to wilt or are air dried

2) dried in an oven at 80 Deg. C.

3) placed in boiling water

4) placed in boiling water and then dried in an oven at 80 Deg. C.

then at least 75% of the isatan B precursor of indigo is lost. This will correspondingly reduce the amount of indigo which can be produced by about 50%. This problem does not arise with the Polygonum tinctoria or Indigofera plant as the only precursor to indigo in these plants is indican which is not affected.

Recent research also indicates that there is much more indigo in the centre of the dried woad balls than there is at the outer surface of the balls. It seems that all the available precursor material in the woad leaves is converted to indigo at the chopping or grinding stage of making the woad ball. The more thoroughly the leaves are macerated and mixed the more of the precursor is converted to indigo. The efficiency of the process is greatly dependant on the initial grinding and mixing of the freshly gathered woad leaves. At the time Jamieson Hurry wrote his book in the 1930's, it was not appreciated that two precursors were present (indican or indoxyl-B-D-glucoside and isatan B or indoxyl-5-ketoglutinate) and that 80% was in the form of isatan B.

According to the research by Prof. Meyer(21) the bacteria responsible for the breakdown of the Indigo precursors in woad is mainly Enterobacter agglomerans which occurs naturally on the woad leaf

Initially on macerating the leaves the bacteria rapidly increase, with indigo production increasing rapidly after about 4 days. The enzymes produced cleaves the indoxyl from its glucoside or ketoglutinate which serves as a growth substrate for the bacteria. The indoxyl combines with oxygen from the air to give indigo. This process can take up to 19 days. It appears that one type of bacteria (E. agglomerans) is responsible for the conversion of the woad precursors to indigo in the chopped leaves, woad ball stage and couching stage. Further research is being undertaken at Reading University in the Department of Plant Sciences on this subject(4).

For indigo to be formed from the sap of the woad leaf, the molecules of indoxyl must be separated from the isatan and indican by the action of enzymes (formed by E. agglomerans). These indoxyl molecules then recombine together to give indigo.

In the final stage when hot water and alkali are added to the woad vat, the released indigo must be redissolved by fermentation for the purpose of dyeing the cloth. To redissolve the indigo to leuco indigo it is reduced by bacterial action or chemically with a reducing agent at pH 9 and 60 Deg. C. in the vat, by the removal of oxygen. This reaction in the vat takes about 30 hours to complete.

Wetted natural fibre can then be placed in the vat, but protected from the woad sludge at the bottom of the vat with a net. After 30 minutes or so, as the saturated cloth is finally lifted out of the vat, the oxygen of the air rapidly oxidises the green coloured leuco-indigo to the characteristic blue indigo which is then fixed to the cloth.

17th. Century. Celia Feines Description(22) of a Woad Mill

In about 1700 Celia Fiennes, a lady with aristocratic connections, took it upon herself to travel the length and breadth of England on horseback, staying at stately homes and happily maintaining a diary of her experiences. This was of course at that time an intrepid undertaking for anyone and particularly a lady. Her diary now provides a valuable insight to life at that time. She describes a visit to a woad mill at Toddington in Bedfordshire in 1694. This description does provide a glimpse of the method of growing and processing woad in England in the 17th. and 18th. centuries. This was a method whereby itinerant "contractors" would maintain a permanent team of woad workers and their families. They would travel from parish to parish in the midlands and would lease from the local landowners a number of acres taken over from a tenant farmer for two or three years for the purpose of growing and processing the woad crop to the ball stage. This provision was frequently written into the tenant farmers leases.

Celia relates :- "I saw some of the land improved in the production of woads which the dyers use; its ordered in this manner, all the Summer season if dry for 4 or 5 months they sow it or plant it (but I think it is sown) then it is very clean weeded, when grown up a little out of the ground for it rises no higher than lettuce and much in such tuffts, the colour of the leaves is much like scabious and the shape resembling that, this they cut off close to the ground and so out of the same root springs the leaf again. This they do 4 times then in a mill with a horse they grind the leaves into a paste, so make it up into balls and dry them in a penthouse to secure it from rain, only the wind dries it; this plantation of about 12 acres would employ 2 or 3 families men, women and children, and so they generally come and make little huts for themselves for the season to tend it.

Here I saw flax in growth, the smell of the woad is so strong and offensive; you can scarce bear it at the mill; I could not force my horse near it."

The woad fields required careful hand weeding before gathering the leaves to avoid mixing woad with weeds which the dyers said would "sadden the dye".

19th Century Woad Growing in England 1813 (23)

The method of cultivating this plant, and the advantages to be derived from it, have been so well fully explained by A. Young Esq. in his Survey of Lincolnshire that it will not be necessary to attempt it here.

"At Newport Pagnell, Mr Ward has let 25 acres of pasture to Mr Neale of Watford in Northamptonshire, to grow woad for four years successively upon sward, after being, in the first instance, pared and burnt. Mr Neale brings his own servants with him; and a spot of ground near the land which he hires, he erects a millhouse and mill for bruising the woad, as soon as it is cut and carried from the ground where it grows; and near this house are huts, built of turf and wood, for the families which he brings with him. Here they remain as a colony for four years, during which time they look out for another portion of sward land, to be cultivated in the same manner. Much of this woad prepared by Mr Neale is sent to Norwich."

The Demise of Woad

Despite great opposition from the vested interests of the woad growers and merchants on the continent of Europe, the end of the woad trade as a staple of international trade was sealed with the arrival in Europe of refined indigo from India. This came about with the opening of the sea route to the East first by the Portuguese navigators and subsequently exploited by the British East India Company. Still extant in the Public Record Office (20), is the memorandum dated the 27th April 1577 sent by the representatives of the merchants and dyers of the City of London to the Privy Council requesting permission to use the newly imported indigo from India via Portugal, in the woad vats to produce a cheaper more "oryent" blue.

"Whereas one Pero Vas Devora Portoguese is sente from the King of Portogale into this Realme to make shewe and triall of the working of a certein commodity or merchantise named Aneel commonly called in English Blue ynde which cometh out of the East yndias and by report is made of the flower and first croppe and cutte of an herb growing there whereof woad is made not before this tyme practized uppon wull or clothe in England.

The said Pero Vas hath accordinglie shewed howe to use and occupie the same, to us the diars and merchants hereunder named and others, several tymes in the citie of London, being putt and set to worke with certein quantitie of woade in the common woade fats used in London whiche have wrought kindlie and duelie toguether, and have perfite and durable colour of Blue, Azure and Watchets according to the nature of good woade. And the commoditie that wee do finde by the same Aneel is that fortie shillings bestowed in the same, yeldeth as much colour as fiftie shillings in woade, or (for a more plain understanding) iiij li waighte (4 pounds weight) of the same prised at fortie shillings, yeldeth as much colour to our judgement as one hundreth weight of Tholose woade nowe worth fiftie shillings and maketh more oryent colour, and we saie that uppon this triall the same commoditie will and maie hereafter be occupied in this citie uppon cloth, and it will be profitable in divers respects, if it be had at reasonable price, but we esteem it to be too deer at X ss. the pounde, for that woade will fall of the price that now is, god sending more quiet tyme.

Also the said Pero Vas saieth that he is readie to shewe the proof of the same Aneel upon wulls unwroughte if he be sent to places in the cuntrie where it is most used and affirmeth that it is more profitable and goeth further and it will be better liked to die wulls unwroughte, which is most commonlie used through all Englande.

dated in London the xxvii the day of Aprile 1577.
By me Robert Dow
By me Rychard Nay
By me Donston Ames
By me John Bayly dyere
By me Rychard Cooper dyer
By me William Glover dyer"

From the beginning there was no opposition to the use of imported Indian indigo in England. This was in marked contrast to the reaction in France and Germany where woad growing was a large and important industry.

Indigo Dyeing in the 19th. Century

In the 19th. century methods were discovered which allowed indigo to be dissolved in water using purely chemical methods. These were normally used to dye cotton at ambient temperature. These included(26) the iron sulphate, zinc and soda processes with lime as the alkali.. The processes were normally too alkaline to be used with wool.

As part of Arts and Crafts movement William Morris was dyeing cloth in the indigo/woad.

The quotation from the book about William Morris by Elizabeth Wilhide(27) reads as follows:-

In the 1880's it became Morris's custom to display the technique to Merton Abbey visitors, as described by an American guest in 1886:

"In the first outhouse that we entered stood great vats of liquid dye into which some skeins of unbleached wool were dipped for our amusement, as they were brought dripping forth, they appeared of a sea-green colour, but after a few minutes exposure to the air, they settled into a fast, dusky blue."

The sudden transformation of colour from green to blue was evidently a favourite spectacle. The visitor went on to record the orderly atmosphere in the dyehouse and how the smell of dried herbs from the vegetable dyes blended with the fresh country air.

As late as the 1880's woaded cloth was still advertised in the newspaper as a superior form of dyed cloth. Wool continued to be dyed in the indigo/woad vats on a very small scale as late as 1931. According to Hurry(2) this was due to the demand for woaded cloth by the London Metropolitan Police.

Synthetic Indigo

Indigo was not the first of the natural dyes to be made synthetically. Alizarin, the red dye from madder was in fact the first in 1869. This undoubtedly encouraged further efforts to synthesise indigo. Perkins produced his mauveine purple dye by chance in about 1858. This was a synthetic dye but did not duplicate an existing natural dye.

It is estimated that nearly a million pounds(24) at the time was spent in research in Germany before a commercial synthetic indigo was made in 1897.

The excitement, created by this development, with many chemists investigating coal tar dyes at the time, is illustrated by Sherlock Holmes. In the storey of The Empty House, when Holmes was hiding in France to escape the attentions of the master criminal Dr Moriarty, Watson reports Holmes as saying "Returning to France, I spent some months in research into coal-tar derivatives, which I conducted in a laboratory at Montpelier, in the south of France. Having concluded this to my satisfaction,.....". Watson does not relate what wonderful new dyes Holmes must have discovered...

It was in the 1890s when systematic chemistry and the interest in synthetic dyes had advanced sufficiently that the molecular structure of the dyes alizarin, luteolin and indigo were established. Finally Bayer's synthesis of indigo, on a commercial scale, brought about the total collapse of the natural indigo industry in India. In the words of a contemporary artisan, "It's all done by machines now Sir!"

Dyeing with Fresh Woad Leaves

As a practical demonstration or in order to dye on a very small scale, the fresh leaves of the woad plant can be used. Fill a basin with as many fresh first year leaves as it will hold. These can be roughly torn into pieces. Add a handful of washing soda or other alkali and pour on very hot, but not boiling water to fill the basin. Allow this to stand for about 40 minutes and then decant the liquid into another basin. The liquid will be a dark olive green. If it is stirred vigorously at this stage the foam turns blue as the liquid is oxidised to indigo. A teaspoonful of sodium dithionite or "Colour Run Remover" should now be added to the liquid.(note this substance is poisonous and should not be handled by children). The liquid may be gently stirred to mix in the sodium dithionite. This will cause the indigo to dissolve giving a greenish colour. Cloth of natural fibre should be first wetted and then immersed in the liquid for about 30 minutes. When the cloth is withdrawn it will be a green colour and quickly turns blue as the air oxidises it back to indigo which is now fixed to the cloth. Indigo is one of the few natural dyes which does not require a mordant.

To Demonstrate that a Precursor to Indigo Exists in the Woad Leaf

Hurry(2) gives a recipe devised by H.Molisch in 1899 to turn a woad leaf blue. It is necessary to place some fresh woad leaves in a 2 lb. jamjar with a small quantity of ammonia and close with the lid. The sap in the leaves then slowy turns a a dark greenish blue after any time ranging from 24 hours to one week. The leaves can then be removed and placed in a jar full of alcohol or methylated spirits and left for 24 hours. The alcohol removes the green chlorophyl from the leaf. The leaves can then be dried and appear blue when held up to the light. The treated leaves are extremely brittle. They should be lifted out with tweezers and dropped into warm water to soften them. They can then be pressed like dried flowers and be preserved between sheets of transparent plastic.

References

1. Gioanventura Rossetti, The Plictho, The 1548 edition translated by S.M.Edelstein and H.C.Borghetty.
2. Dr Jamieson B. Hurry, The Woad Plant and Its Dye, 1930. Reprinted by Augustus M. Kelly, Clifton.
3. Dominique Cardon, Guide des Teinture Naturelles, 1990 pub. Delachaux et Niestle, Switzerland.
4. Professor Philip John, Plant Sciences Dept. Reading University.
5. The Recipe for the woad vat of the Arte Della Lana in Florence (1418). See Proc. of the 1995 Woad Conference, Toulouse.
6. Mini Dictionary of Chemistry, Oxford University Press 1988.
7. J. Hellot, L'Art de la teinture des laines et des etoffes de laine en grand et petit teint. Paris 1750.
8. E. Bancroft, Experimental Researches concerning the Philosophy of Permanent Colours. London 1794.
9. Elijah Bemiss, The Dyer's Companion. 1815.
10. William Partridge, A Practical Treatise on Dying. 1823. Republished by the Pasold Research Fund Ltd. 1973.
11. Asa Ellis jun., The Country Dyer's Assistant, Brookfield, Massachussetts, 1798.
12. S.I. Rudenko, Frozen Graves of Siberia, Dent 1970.
13. Bischof, Lecture Toulouse Conference proceedings 1995.
14. Harry Rothwell, English Historical Documents, Vol 3. Pub. by Eyre and Spottiswode.
15. Joan Thirsk, Economic Projects in the 16th. Century. Clarendon Paperbacks.
16. Private correspondence with the author.
17. A.F.Kendrick, Catalogue of Tapestries at the Victoria and Albert Museum, Dept. of Textiles. 1914.
18. Private correspondence with the author
19. Mini Dictionary of Chemistry, Oxford University Press 1988.
20. Letter from the City of London Dyers to the Privy Council re Indigo 1577. Public Record Office.
21. Prof O.Meyer, Bacteriology of the woad fermentation, Toulouse Conference, June 1995.

22. The Illustrated Journeys of Celia Fiennes, 1685-1712, Edited by C. Morris. Macdonald, page 54.
23. Rev. St John Priest, From the General View of the Agriculture of Buckinghamshire, 1813. Printed by Sherwood, Neely and Jones: Chap. 6 Crops Section xxxiv Woad.
24. Mathias Seefelder, Indigo, B.A.S.F.- A.G.(Editor), Ludswighafen 1982.
25. Francis Pritchard, Late Saxon Textiles from the City of London, The Museum of London, Dept. of Urban Archaeology, Offprint 29 from Medieval Archaeol 28 (1984) 46-76.
26. J.J.Hummel - The Dyeing of Textile Fibres,1896
27. Elizabeth Wilhide, William Morris Decor and Design. 1991, pub. Pavilion Books Ltd. (ISBN 1 85793 331 1).

HISTORIC DYES SERIES

New series of booklets on the history of dyeing and methods of dyeing used in the past

These booklets are for those interested in the history of textile dyeing and the details of the methods used by professional dyers in the past using the dyestuffs and technology available to them

Since prehistoric times dyers have been able to produce a wide range of dyed fabrics, limited only by the available technology.

In the dye house of the Chiltern Open Air Museum in Buckinghamshire we are gradually recreating dyed wool, silk and cotton fabrics, which were popular and fashionable in the past. In addition we are researching the history of 18th. century and medieval dyes and the famous imperial purple. A series of booklets are being prepared explaining the history of the natural dyestuffs and the techniques used by the dyers in the past. The first of the series is now available and is devoted to techniques of indigo dyeing using woad. The medieval woad vat has only recently been researched and demonstrated. However archaic the process may be, it is in fact a scientifically efficient and practical method to preserve the indigo in woad leaves and finally to dissolve the indigo to leuco indigo using basic fermentation methods. The last book written on this subject was by Jamieson Hurry in 1931, long before modern scientific analysis could be applied to the subject. This booklet contains practical and scientific information on the woad vat published for the first time.

Copies may be obtained from John Edmonds, 89 Chessfield Park, Little Chalfont, Bucks. HP6 6RX, United Kingdom.

À la recherche de l'indigo perdu

John Edmonds est un de ces sorciers du 20e siècle qui aurait sans doute ètè brûlé vif il y a quelques siécles. Il s'est fait une spécialité de la teinture à partir de plantes. Lors de la fête au village, et parallèlement à l'inauguration du jardin botanique, il expliquait comment il avait retrouvé des techniques perdues depuis longtemps.

Il exposait sur son stand toutes les phases de la fermentation, des feuilles de guède aux grumeaux ou cocagnes de bleu.

Cette manière de faire vivre le jardin des plantes tinctoriales, en relation avec l'atelier de la magnanerie, est des plus vivantes. Elle ne peut que participer au dèveloppement d'un tourisme original dans notre règion.

Nouvelle Republique 5 June 1998

The research into the lost indigo

John Edmonds is one of these wizards of the 20th century that would probably have been burnt at the stake in former centuries. He has made a speciality of dyes from plants. At the time of the fete in the village of Le Coudray Macouard, and at the inauguration of the botanical garden, he explained how he had recovered techniques which had been lost for a long time.

He displayed on his stand all the phases of fermentation, of woad leaves to woad balls and couched woad.

This display brought to life the garden of dye plants, and related to the shop of the Magnanerie. It can only add to the development of an original tourism in our region.

Le Miracle du Bleu

Pour le première fois depuis 6 siècles, on a tient au pastel, ce vendredi, à Toulouse.

En appliquant une recette notée en février 1418.

Tout a commencé la veille, à 10 heures, quand John Edmonds, président de l'association des amis du Musée de plein air de Chiltern, dans les environs de Londres, a entrepris une expérience dans l'atelier de demonstration paralléle au congrès international sur les colorants.

Et à l'heure prévue, reconnaissable à une transformation de l'odeur, John a trempé dans le liquide jaune vert de la cuve une poignée de laine cardée. Qui en est sortie jaune verdâtre.

Puis, à l'air, en quelques dizaines de secondes, s'est transformée en une boule indigo

Et le miracle s'est reproduit sur les écharpes, cravates, T-shirts des congressistes.Hier, pour la première fois depuis 6 siècles, on a teint au pastel, à Toulouse.

Mireille Harrburger,
La Dépêche du Midi 10 June 1995

The Miracle of Blue

For the first time for 6 centuries, woad dyeing is taking place, this Friday, in Toulouse.

A recipe dated to February 1418 was used for this demonstration All began with the vigil, at 10 o'clock, when John Edmonds, chairman of the association of the Friends of the Chiltern Open Air Museum, in the vicinity of London, undertook an experiment in the demonstration hall in parallel with the international convention on colorants.

And at the predicted hour, recognisable by a transformation of the odour, John soaked a handful of carded wool in the green yellow liquid of the vat. It came out a greenish yellow colour.

Then, to air it, in about ten seconds, it changed into an indigo ball. And the miracle was reproduced on the scarves, ties, and T-shirts of the delegates.

Yesterday, for the first time in 6 centuries, woad dyeing took place in Toulouse.